Continued Praise for *You Only Die Once*

"Jeffrey Althaus has an easygoing, humorous way of presenting the difficult topic of estate planning!"

**—Elizabeth Peterson,
Optometrist and Former Client**

"*You Only Die Once* is extremely informative and packed full of fascinating information. Coming from someone who loves to read and learn, law books can be very dry. This is written so you learn an incredible amount of information in a fun, easy way. Estate planning is something that, unless you're an estate guru like Althaus, it's a dark area that people don't know where to begin or what questions to ask to it keeps being postponed for fear of the unknown. This book has certainly cleared up areas that even I wasn't sure about and it made me feel more comfortable knowing what I need and where to start."

—Denise Schilling, Realtor

"Jeffrey Althaus wrote this book with YOU in mind. He made a scary and difficult conversation approachable and light. The content is not stuffy, boring, or filled with fancy legal jargon. It's meant to break estate planning into one simple message – you only die once, so be sure you do it right. For you and your family, so that they can speak positively about the planning you put into place even after you're gone."

—Rosie Garner, Former Client

"I'm in the business of helping folks protect their income and assets and finally I have a resource that says everything I want my customers to understand about preserving their estate! Jeffrey writes with humor, candor, and cold-hard facts, a compelling formula that makes it hard to put down. I'll be recommending this book to all of my customers when we do financial and asset reviews. It's an invaluable tool in my business. Thank you Jeffrey!"

—Tim Brown, State Farm Agent

"I cannot thank Jeffrey Althaus enough for all he did for me after my husband's death. When you are grieving, the last thing you want to do is worry about your estate, probate, and the multitude of legal issues that need to be addressed. His professionalism and especially his compassion during this difficult time helped me to seamlessly get through what could have been a daunting legal process to settle my estate. Jeffrey is highly respected for his legal expertise and knowledge, integrity, honesty and high quality of personalized customer service."

—Debbie Tuttle, Former Client

YOU ONLY DIE ONCE

YOU
ONLY
DIE
ONCE

A Guide to Estate Planning
for You and Your Loved Ones

Jeffrey Althaus, J.D.

To contact the author directly, please visit: https://althauslaw.com

Disclaimer: All former clients and reviewers gave permission to use their name and feedback on the book.

Printed in the United States of America

ISBN Paperback: 978-1-947341-36-4
ISBN eBook: 978-1-947341-37-1

Library of Congress Control Number: 2018953399

Cover Design: Redwood Publishing, LLC
Interior Design: Ghislain Viau

Table of Contents

Intro — Odds Are, You're Only Going to Die Once

L et's play the odds and pretend it's inevitable that you are going to die. Someday—not that long from now, when you think about it—you're going to keel over, become kaput, and push up daisies, all those wonderful euphemisms I hear all too frequently in my profession. Any way you put it, there is a 100 percent chance of your calling it quits eventually.

Yet almost no one on the planet wants to talk about it, or in any way be prepared, until it's too late. All of us are just walking around like invincible super heroes set to live forever, or at least pass away centuries from now with absolutely zero problems until that day comes. And when it comes? Well, obviously, we go from perfectly fine, fully functioning human beings with all our cognitive abilities intact, to . . . just gone, passed in our sleep, most likely. Afterward, everyone we want to inherit our things just magically gets everything we wanted them to.

That scenario happens to virtually no one. That's right, next to zero percent.

While we only die once, most people are extremely under-prepared for it. **Yet we *all* have access to *everything* we need to plan for our death.** We don't even have to talk to a lawyer to do it. Simply having a conversation with family and friends while putting our wishes down on paper is better than nothing! But many of us don't even do that.

Here are some statistics revealing how many of us are extremely underprepared for the inevitable:

- **50%** of people don't have a medical power of attorney in place. This means there is absolutely no one who can speak to a doctor regarding whether or not you want your leg chopped off if you are in a coma. You've got another one anyway, right? (1)

- **55%** of people don't have any type of estate planning in place. This includes even just a simple will. You're fine with the state deciding who gets your things, right? Taxes? Nope, definitely didn't pay enough of those! (2)

- **78%** of adults under the age of thirty-six do not have a will. This includes people with children! The *only* surefire way to prevent foster care for your kids is to appoint a guardian for them in your estate plan. (3)

- **32%** of Americans say they would rather have a root canal, pay taxes, or give up sex instead of talking about their estate planning. REALLY?! I am *clearly* not doing my taxes right. (4)

- **22%** of people feel as though they don't need an estate plan at all. This means they believe that their spouse or family will be able to make decisions for them or inherit their stuff without a plan in place. This is a smaller number, but an amazing misconception. This one is just not true. (5)

- Most people say they want to pass at home, yet only **26%** have a health-care directive saying so. (6)

Here are some of the consequences of not having an estate plan:

- Everything you've worked hard for could literally go to the state. I don't know anyone who likes taxes that much.

- Your children could be left with nothing. This is especially true for people involved in second or third marriages. Here's an example: A is married to B. They have kids. A dies, so all A's stuff goes to B. B remarries C later in life. B dies, and all B's stuff (including A's stuff because A had no plan) goes to C. C goes to live on a beach in Hawaii. The children get nothing—not a thing.

- If you own a business and don't have a financial power of attorney, there will be no one to make decisions for your company, pay bills, access bank accounts, or keep your clients happy. There goes your business. It wasn't that important, was it?

- Heck, if you own anything and become incapacitated without a power of attorney in place, your things could vanish by the time you regain capacity. Mortgage payments, water bills, car payments—who pays those if you are in a coma?

- Your children could go to foster care. Appointing a guardian for them now stops that. I don't know what else to say about it; that's pretty powerful.

- Your money could go to paying a professional you've never met to manage your things. Let me reiterate: you *do not know this person* and you have to pay them an *exorbitant amount of money* to make decisions for you.

So, we've played the numbers and looked at some stats. Here's another one people don't think about and rarely plan for: while you will only die once, you will likely become incapacitated multiple times throughout your life.

Who makes decisions for you then?

Without a plan, the court, that's who. Some judge who hasn't met you or your family will appoint a "professional" who hasn't met you and doesn't know you at all to manage your finances and/or your health-care decisions. This means someone you've never even talked to could decide to keep you on life support indefinitely or pull the plug.

Again, a "professional" you do not know will be appointed and you'll have to pay that person. A lot. So there goes the inheritance you thought you'd be giving your kids.

But I don't have an "estate."

I'm just going to go ahead and call bull on this one. Every single person has an estate. Maybe not the size of Warren Buffett's, but we all have something. Consider the following:

- **Debt:** Didn't think this one counted, eh? Well it does. Your debt doesn't just vanish when you die. Not even a lot of student loans go away. Have a cosigner on your loan? Those people are stuck paying your bills if you pass with no plan. Have credit card debt or private student loans? Someone still has to pay those. Only federal student loans are eligible to be automatically discharged on death.

- **Family heirlooms:** I realize this is an ancient term, but everyone has stuff that is important to them. Maybe you got a watch from your grandpa. Maybe you have your great-grandmother's wedding ring. Heck, maybe you have a Picasso. The point is, everyone has something important to them that they would like to have stay in the family and not get eaten by a crow in some landfill somewhere.

- **Last wishes:** This isn't technically property, but you have the right to decide what happens to you when you pass away. Without a plan, you give up that right. More importantly, you throw this enormous burden on your loved ones who *will* be unprepared for it. One study showed that when asked how their spouse wanted to be treated in certain medical situations, spouses guessed wrong 60% of the time.

- **Children:** This is a big one. I can't tell you how many people come through my doors with children and don't have a guardian lined up to care for their kids if something should happen to them. Here's a fact for you: spouses travel *together.* They get in accidents *together.* If nothing is in place, they have left their kids to the care of the state *together.* This one is so easy to solve and your children are the most important things in your life, period.

Why does no one want to talk about the inevitable? After seeing the stats and knowing what could happen without an estate plan, it seems like a no-brainer. But it's not. **The hard truth of the matter is that talking about the end of your life isn't easy—but it's necessary. The pain and anguish caused by not doing it are too costly.** I get the point of view that some people have: "Just throw me away with the trash," or "I'm dead; what do I care?" If it were that easy—no one else was impacted by your death and no one fought about it afterward—then maybe those thoughts would be fine. The truth, however, is that many people can be impacted by your death. (Also, we don't throw bodies out, in case you were wondering. That's illegal.)

Throughout this book, we will dive deep into the most common strategies and tools to properly execute estate planning. This isn't meant to encourage you to go out and pay huge amounts of money to get a full-blown estate plan with all the bells and whistles. It is simply to inform you of the horror stories I have witnessed in my career, and spread the word about a little-known area of law called estate planning.

When people don't know about estate planning, it truly can wreak havoc on lives. So, go have the talk with your family. Stop putting it off. You don't have to call me, but please call an estate-planning attorney somewhere. Most of us offer a free consultation so you can bear being in the same room with a lawyer for a bit. **The moral of the story is *do something*.** You don't have to get a root canal or give up sex. Please don't do that.

The numbers all point to the ball being in your court to protect the ones you love.

What Is Estate Planning?

So, what in the world is estate planning, anyway? It's an overarching term that encompasses a lot of different things. These things include the following:

- Wills
- Trusts
- Financial Powers of Attorney
- Medical Powers of Attorney
- Living Wills and Other Advance Care Directives
- Health Insurance Portability and Accountability Act (HIPAA) releases
- Personal Property Memoranda
- Declaration of Final Remains Document
- And More

Estate planning is a category of documents that—together—help protect your assets and your family members both while you are alive and after you pass away. In addition to security and protection, these documents also help you get your things where you want them to go eventually. Don't understand what all these documents do? That's OK. We're getting to that.

Protecting Your Assets

How will an estate plan help you to protect your assets? You spend a lifetime working hard and building your estate. **It's worth protecting.** Few people wake up in the morning and think, "Gee, I really hope the state takes all my stuff away from me today." In reality, without proper planning, this *could* happen to you. By putting the right documents in place, you ensure that your family and your assets are safeguarded for the long term.

We will get to the exact definition of wills and powers of attorney shortly. For now, know that a will lets you declare where you want your things to go. This helps you prevent the unfortunate situation in which a second husband (or wife) ends up with all of the first husband's (or wife's) assets, preventing the kids from receiving an inheritance.

Powers of attorney help protect your things while you are still alive. By naming an agent to act for you in certain situations, you are safeguarded from having a random guardian or conservator appointed for you. **It's vital to know that if you do not have an estate plan, the state *will* write one for**

you and charge you handsomely. This doesn't mean that the state sits down and drafts all the documents with an attorney. It means that instead of having your own power of attorney, the state appoints professionals to make those decisions for you, and you pay them a lot of money to do so. This is a large burden to put on your family. It has driven people broke, yet it's easily preventable.

Protecting Your Family

One way estate planning helps protect your family is by making sure they get the property you want them to receive. Planning also protects them in other ways. Through certain types of trusts, you are able to monitor when children will receive money and how much money they will receive—even after you are gone. You can decide if that inheritance should be spent on school, medical expenses, or a place to live. You can even help to buy a new car, and all of this after you have passed away.

One of the most important ways an estate plan protects your family members is by taking very stressful decisions out of their hands. For instance, if you have a valid living will, your family will not have to decide whether or not to keep you on life support if you are in a vegetative state. Your living will decides that for them. *I cannot stress enough how difficult a decision that is to make for someone else.* Those who have had to make it for others understand that signing the document that terminates life support for your loved one is one of the toughest decisions you may ever face. Putting a living will in place stops that situation from happening because you have already decided for your family. They won't have to do so.

Further, having a will and proper supporting documents takes other stressful decisions away from your loved ones. They won't have to guess where you wanted things to go. They won't have to decide if you wanted a funeral, where you want to be buried, or if you would rather be cremated. You will have laid out neatly all those decisions in a legally binding plan. That takes the stressful choices away from your family so they can mourn properly without worrying about the legal stuff.

A properly drafted estate plan can do some pretty amazing things. It just takes the right kind of knowledge and the desire to protect the ones you love.

Putting It All Together

An estate plan isn't just for those with millions of dollars. It's for anyone who wants to secure their assets and protect their family. It can help answer questions such as:

- Where will my things go if something happens to me?
- Will the mortgage be paid?
- Who will watch over my children?
- What happens to my things and my family if I become incapacitated?

- Who will be in charge of my estate?

- Will my things go through probate?

- Will I owe any taxes?

There are many estate-planning documents in a full package, all of which work together to help provide you and your family with the most protections possible. A skilled estate-planning lawyer can help guide you down the right path to make sure you and your loved ones are set for whatever the future brings.

Basic Estate-Planning Documents Explained to a Six-Year-Old

"If you can't explain it to a six-year-old,
you don't understand it yourself."
— Albert Einstein

The point of this chapter is understanding. I take the above quote from good ol' Al seriously—*especially* when it comes to estate planning. I can't tell you how many times people have told me that they get the basics of estate planning, but when we get down to the nitty-gritty, they admit they misunderstood many of the tools and their usefulness. **Misunderstanding estate planning is not something about which to be embarrassed or ashamed.** It is a much more complex and in-depth topic than people realize.

Yet grasping the core concepts can be quite simple if properly explained. Simple explanations here will allow us to move on to the more advanced topics later.

The following explanations of estate documents are meant to give a baseline understanding of each. Keep in mind, we will cover each of these documents in more detail in later chapters. Please bear with me since these conversations can get a tad morbid. It's just the nature of estate planning. Not many people *like* talking about it, but we do because it's necessary to protect our loved ones.

Moving forward, please be aware that I will be using the words "attorney" and "lawyer" interchangeably. That is because they mean the exact same thing in the United States.

The Last Will and Testament

First up is the will. This is the bread-and-butter estate-planning document; no plan is complete without one. So how do you explain a will to a six-year-old? Here goes:

Six-Year-Old: "Mommy, Daddy, what's a will?"

Parent: "A will is a stack of papers in which Mommy and Daddy get to decide who gets all of their stuff when they pass away."

That's it. That's all you have to say. Let's pretend this six-year-old is an *actual* six-year-old and has some follow-up questions:

Six-Year-Old: "But why?"

Parent: "Well, you like our house and your things, don't you? We decide now what happens to everything because we want to make sure you are safe and still have toys to play with and a roof over your head when you are older."

We won't get into the details here of how your things can go to unintended people or to the state, but for now, just know they can.

Parents with minor children should also be thinking about guardianship. Maybe your child throws you this curveball:

Six-Year-Old: "But is that really all a will does?"

Parent: "I'm glad you asked. Mommy and Daddy also get to name the people who will take care of you and raise you to be big and strong if we aren't around to do that anymore."

That's the plain and simple point of naming a guardian for your kids. If you aren't able to be there anymore—you are incapacitated or have passed away—then who raises your children? **If you don't name someone, that could mean they'll go to foster care or end up with a relative you would never want to raise them.**

There you have it. A will does two main things*:

1. Allows you to declare where you want your stuff to go when you die.

2. Allows you to name a guardian for your children.
   *A will does more than this, but that is for later chapters.

Trust

This one is more complicated to fully understand, but the basics are almost identical to a will. So why do you need a trust *and* a will? Great question! You may not. Let's learn a little more:

> *Six-Year-Old:* "Mommy, Daddy, what's a trust?" (I've heard kids ask crazier questions, so just roll with it.)

> *Parent:* "Well, honey, a trust is a big stack of papers that lets Mommy and Daddy decide where all their stuff goes when they pass away."

Wait a minute. Hold the phone. That's exactly what a will does! What are you trying to pull here?

> *Six-Year-Old:* "Ummmm . . . you just said that's what a will does. I don't get it."

> *Parent:* "You're paying attention. Good job! A trust is a much bigger stack of papers than a will. It also starts protecting you and all these things around you *immediately*. Our will doesn't start working until we are gone."

So that's the main difference: a trust starts working now instead of later, like a will. There are a lot more pages to a trust, and those pages have terms in them that allow the trust to take effect immediately—whereas a will is more of a "back-burner document" in that we don't usually look at it until you pass away. Trusts also cost a lot more and take more administrative work to get set up properly. We will get into the intricacies of trusts later; for instance, trusts also let you avoid probate. We haven't yet explained probate to our six-year-old, so hold on to that nugget. For now, just know this:

Trusts

1. Let you declare where you want your stuff to go when you die.

2. Start protecting your stuff and your family immediately—not later, like a will.

3. Allow you to avoid probate (unlike a will).

Guardianship

Next up is the guardianship for minor children. Before we dive into this one, you must know that there are also guardianship proceedings for adults when they become incapacitated. That is not what we are explaining to our six-year-old here. We are simply talking about naming a guardian for minor children so if both parents pass away, or are otherwise hurt, there is someone to take care of their kids. Here goes:

Six-Year-Old: "Mommy, Daddy, what happens to me if you guys aren't around anymore?"

Parent: "We took steps to make sure you are protected no matter what happens to us, darling. We named people, called your 'guardians,' to make sure you have a place to live, food to eat, and a school to go to. And don't worry, it's not Aunt Thelma; we know you hate it when she pinches your cheek."

There you have it. Naming a guardian allows you to declare who will have custody of your children if something happens to you. People don't like to think about it, but spouses travel together, spend a lot of time together, and therefore get in accidents together. What happens if you do not name a guardian to care for your children? A judge you have never met will be forced to guess who would be the best parent for your child. This means that a relative you may never want raising your kids could end up with them. It also means that your children could end up in foster care.

Six-Year-Old: "But you said you named Uncle Jim and Aunt Lisa as my godparents. Won't they take care of me?"

Parent: "As your godparents, Uncle Jim and Aunt Lisa play a different role. We always want them guiding you down the right path, but your legal guardian has nothing to do with who your godparents are."

This one is critical. **Many people falsely assume that since they have named godparents, or had some side conversation with relatives, that they have fulfilled their duty as a parent of protecting their children.** THIS IS NOT TRUE. The court does not give children to godparents simply because they have been named as godparents. *You must name a legal guardian.* That is the only way to make sure your children have a home with the people you want them to have a home with. Furthermore, this is the best way to make sure your children don't go to foster care should something happen to you.

So, let's sum it up. Guardianships allow you to do the following:

1. Name an individual or set of people to care for your children if you can't anymore.

2. Provide the best path to preventing your children from going to an unintended relative or foster care.

Financial Power of Attorney

There are two types of powers of attorney, financial and medical. Let's see what our six-year-old has to say:

Six-Year-Old: "Mommy, Daddy, what's a financial power of attorney?"

Parent: "Great question, sweetie! A financial power of attorney allows us to name a person who will take care of all our money if we are hurt."

Powers of attorney allow you to name an agent to act for you if you become incapacitated. Once you pass away, however, powers of attorney are no longer valid and your will takes over how your property will be distributed. Your financial power of attorney is in charge of all financial decisions that you currently make *should you become incapacitated*. They can't override your decisions while you have capacity; they can only act once a doctor says you are incapacitated (unless you choose otherwise).

Six-Year-Old: "But what's the point?"

Parent: "Well, if we don't name someone now, a stranger may have to come in and manage all our stuff for us. This stranger would access our bank accounts and have control over all our property."

Stranger danger! **If you do not name a financial power of attorney now, and then you become incapacitated, *it will be too late to name one.*** What happens next? Without a proper agent in place, the court appoints a professional (called a conservator) to manage your assets. We will dive deeper into this unfortunate scenario later in this book. Just keep in mind it is *not* good and it is *very* costly (multiple thousands of dollars) if the court must step in for whatever reason.

So, let's sum it up. A financial power of attorney allows you to do the following:

1. Appoint an individual to manage your money and assets if you can't anymore.

2. Prevent the court from appointing a conservator to manage your assets, saving you thousands of dollars.

Medical Power of Attorney

A medical power of attorney is very similar:

Six-Year-Old: "Mommy, Daddy, what's a medical power of attorney?"

Parent: "Another great question, dear. A medical power of attorney lets Mommy and Daddy appoint a person who can talk to doctors if we are hurt."

Your medical power of attorney is in charge of all medical decisions that you currently have the ability to make. Like a financial power of attorney, he or she can't override your decisions while you have capacity, and can only act once a doctor says you are incapacitated (assuming that is the choice you make in the document).

Six-Year-Old: "But what's the point?"

Parent: "Well, if we don't name someone now, a stranger may have to come in and talk to our doctors for us. This stranger could be the one deciding whether we live or die and how the doctors will fix us."

Stranger danger . . . again! **If you do not appoint a medical power of attorney now, and then you become incapacitated, it will be too late to name one.** What happens next? Without a proper agent in place, the court will appoint a professional (called a guardian) to make your health-care decisions. Again, we will dive deeper into this unfortunate scenario later in this book. Just bear in mind, it is *not* good and it is *very* costly (thousands of dollars to pay the professional guardian on top of the thousands to have the conservator appointed) if the court must step in for whatever reason.

So, let's sum it up. Medical powers of attorney allow you to do the following:

1. Appoint an individual to talk to doctors and make medical decisions for you if you can't anymore.

2. Prevent the court from appointing a guardian to manage your health-care decisions, saving you thousands of dollars.

Living Will

Next up is the living will. The name of this document is confusing because it is not actually a will at all. It's an **advance directive for medical and surgical treatment**. Why is it called a living will? Good question. I guess lawyers just like to confuse people.

Six-Year-Old: "What is a living will?"

Parent: "It's a piece of paper that allows us to decide whether or not we want to remain on life support in an end-of-life situation."

While this seems very simple, it is also extremely important. This is likely a conversation you haven't had with many people, if any at all. If you actually sit down and think about it, it may be a tough choice for you. It is for many people. Do you want to withdraw life support immediately? Do you want to stay on life support long enough so family can have enough time to say a final good-bye? Do religious factors weigh into your decision?

In the end, this has proven over and over again to be *the most important document* I have ever drafted for my clients. We will get into more details later, but just know that a living will helps to relieve your family members from having to make an extremely stressful decision. The document lets *you* decide how you want to be treated while you have capacity to do so.

So, let's sum it up. Living wills allow you to do the following:

1. Choose how long you would like to be on life support in an end-of-life situation.

2. Take that extremely stressful, difficult decision out of your family's hands.

Probate

The final term we will explain to our six-year-old is probate. Let's dive right in:

Six-Year-Old: "Mommy, Daddy, what is probate?"

Parent: "Well, sweetie, probate is the process most individuals go through after they pass away. It allows the courts to legally allow their property to be transferred to the people they intended to receive it. Most times, you don't even have to go to court."

Many people think of probate as a scary and expensive process that must be avoided. With recent changes to the law, however, probate in most states is simple and quick compared to what it used to be.

Six-Year-Old: "What happens in probate?"

Parent: "Great question! There are a few main things that happen in the probate process:

- The personal representative (person in charge) finds all the assets of the person who passed away.

- That same person then values all the assets of the deceased person.

- All creditors with approved claims are paid and dealt with.

- All property is distributed to the people named in the will."

Six-Year-Old: "But how does property actually get transferred? Does a judge do it?"

Parent: "Most times, a judge doesn't need to be involved much at all. The person in charge is responsible for drafting all the necessary paperwork to ensure property passes to those who are supposed to receive it. The court then signs off on everything done correctly, and you are finished."

The probate process is usually wrapped up within six months. While certain states still have older laws that make probate drag on and become expensive, most states have done away with those laws.

There is one last question your six-year-old has:

Six-Year-Old: "So do people always have to go through probate when they die?"

Parent: "Not always. If people have less than $66,000 (in Colorado in 2018) in their name alone, they can avoid probate. However, if they own a house, they still have to go through probate. Having a trust also allows you to avoid probate."

Each state has a different threshold under which probate can be avoided. In Colorado, it is currently $66,000, but that number is subject to change each year. If any real estate is owned by the decedent, that property must go through probate according to the law.

So, let's sum it up. Probate is the following:

1. The process individuals go through after passing away in order to transfer title of their assets to their heirs or devisees (the people named in a will).

2. Not necessary if you have less than $66,000 in your name alone (this number varies by state and changes each year) and do not own any real estate. It is also not necessary if you have a properly funded trust.

So there you have it: simple explanations of the most common and important terms involved in estate planning. The goal here is to set a foundation that we can build upon in the later chapters. If you ever forget the building blocks of the documents, just refer back here for a quick refresher. The next page includes a one-sheet breakdown so you don't have to reread the entire chapter each time you have a simple question.

One-Sheet Breakdown

I like to make things easy on people, so here's one page that provides simple explanations of each document:

Will

1. Lets you say where you want your stuff to go when you die.

2. Lets you name a guardian for your children.

3. Allows you to name a personal representative to handle probate (discussed more later).

Trust

1. Lets you say where you want your stuff to go when you die.

2. Protects your stuff and your family immediately—not later, like a will.

3. Allows you to avoid probate (unlike a will).

Guardianship

1. Allows you to name an individual or set of people to care for your children if you can't anymore.

2. Is the best way to prevent your children from going to foster care.

Financial Power of Attorney

1. Names an individual to manage your money and assets if you can't anymore.

2. Prevents the court from appointing a professional, called a conservator, to manage your assets.

Medical Power of Attorney

1. Names an individual to talk to doctors and make medical decisions for you if you can't anymore.

2. Prevents the court from appointing a professional, called a guardian, to manage your health-care decisions.

Living Will

1. Allows you to choose how many days you would like to be on life support in an end-of-life situation.

2. Takes that extremely stressful, difficult decision out of your family's hands.

Probate

1. Is the process individuals go through after passing away in order to transfer title of their assets to their heirs.

2. Is not necessary if you have less than $66,000 in your name alone (this number varies by state and changes each year) and do not own any real estate, or if you have a properly funded trust.

The Four Documents Every Person Should Have — A Deeper Explanation

You now understand a little bit more about estate planning and a have a solid overview of what most of the documents actually mean. Now let's dive a little deeper into the big ones and why you need them. There are four main documents everyone should have in their arsenal:

1. Last Will and Testament

2. Living Will

3. Medical Power of Attorney

4. Financial Power of Attorney

Let's break down each one and find out why they are so important.

1. Wills

Wills are the first line of defense when protecting your property and family. **By having an estate-planning attorney draft a complete will, you can help to guarantee that your things will end up with your loved ones, rather than being turned over to the government or passing to unintended individuals.**

A will is an excellent tool that allows you to say exactly what you want to have happen with your property when you pass away. If you don't say anything, the laws of the state where you live take over and decide where your assets will be distributed. This can result in some very unintended consequences.

Let's look a little closer at the example I gave earlier in which your children *possibly receive nothing* when you pass away. If you need a refresher on the setup, I won't make you flip back. Here it is:

A is married to B. They have kids. A dies, so all A's stuff goes to B. B remarries C later in life. B dies, and all B's stuff (including A's stuff because A had no plan) goes to C. C goes to live on a beach in Hawaii. The children get nothing—not a thing.

This scenario is devastating. Sadly, it's much more common than you would think . . . a result of the fact that people don't like to think about it or plan for it because it involves them being six feet under.

The basic concept is this: If you are married without a plan of any kind in place, your stuff will go to your spouse (typically). When you pass away, the odds are in favor of your spouse remarrying. When he or she passes away, your stuff then goes to the new spouse. **This leaves your kids out of the picture completely.** There are some skimpy laws that attempt to protect your children, but they do a poor job of it. **The best way to ensure your children inherit is to have an estate plan.**

Your estate becomes more complex if you have children from different marriages, own property jointly with another individual, or co-own a business with someone else. In these situations, your spouse may not get as much, or may get nothing at all. This is an exception that provides enough information for me to write a whole second book! Maybe one day, but for now, let's stick with the basics.

Let's look at the example above with a simple plan in place. A and B have a plan that says when A dies, things go into a trust for the children, but B can take advantage of the assets while B is still alive. Now, A can pass away and B can marry whomever B pleases. When B dies, the trust will control.

This same result can also be accomplished with a tool known as a "contract to will": both spouses agree that when one spouse dies, the other spouse will never change his or her will. This means that the kids can't ever be accidentally cut out, and the new spouse, if any, will not take their inheritance from them.

The above examples of different asset-protection options are just a few ways that a will or trust can help you to protect your family. There are many more examples of how you and your family can benefit from having a plan in place. Let's dive in and see what they are.

What happens if you have a family heirloom that is deeply important to you? Maybe you have grandpa's old Army pistol or another relative's fine china. Perhaps there is a wedding ring that has been in your family for generations. **A will is the perfect place to list these items to make sure they go to the person you want to have them.** If you fail to do so, the odds are that the item will be liquidated either to pay debts or to distribute cash to your heirs. This is especially true if no one else knows the value of the items you have. Even if everyone knows the value, there is no guarantee that item will get where you want it to go without a properly drafted will.

Another important advantage of a will is the ability to appoint a person called your **personal representative** (formerly known as an executor or executrix). **This is the person you trust to run the entire probate process and make sure your assets are properly distributed per your wishes.** Since you are the one who puts this person in charge, you know you can trust them to do a good job. If you maybe don't *completely* trust them—or just worry that they may need help—you can give them authority to hire a lawyer to help them through the process. The laws have changed to make hiring a lawyer much more cost-effective for your estate.

Your will also allows you to name a guardian for any minor children you have. It's worth repeating that this is absolutely the best way to avoid foster care for your kids. What happens when you do not name a guardian? Your family, if there is anyone who survives you, has to go to court and appear in front of a judge. That judge has the option to name a court-appointed guardian to care for the best interests of your children. That could mean a multitude of things. It could be that a surviving family member is made guardian. It could mean that a professional you have never met is made guardian. Or it could mean that your kids become wards of the state (it all depends on where you live). The bottom line is that putting something in place now prevents the unknown from happening. It lets you decide exactly what will happen and who will parent your children.

The guardianship aspect of a will is why parents who have minor children are the people most in need of an estate plan. Simply putting one in place can turn so many uncertainties into certainties.

2. Living Wills

We learned earlier that living wills allow you say what will happen to you in an end-of-life situation— otherwise known as an "advance health-care directive" or the "pull the plug" document. (Morbid, I know. But you're reading an estate-planning book, so you're probably used to it by now!)

So when does the living will kick in? Very rarely. Two doctors have to say that you no longer have any brain activity (are brain dead), you cannot communicate at all (not even by blinking), and those doctors have the belief that you will never have brain activity or be able to communicate again. Basically, they think you are completely brain dead. When all of these factors have been met, then your living will is pulled out to be examined. That is the only time your living will should be looked at for the purpose of utilizing it.

The important point is that when a living will is needed, it is *the most important document you can have in your plan.* This is my opinion, but no one has been able to convince me otherwise. While it may be easy to toss around the phrases, "I don't want any heroics" or "Just pull the plug and get it over with," actually being the person in the room with you when the time comes is a different story. Having to sign a document that makes the hospital take you off life-sustaining procedures is possibly the hardest decision one of your loved ones will ever have to make.

This document stops anyone from ever having to sign that paper. *You* can decide *now* how you want to be treated, which takes that extremely stressful decision away from everyone else. **I tell my clients all the time that this document is more for**

other people in your life than it is for you. Sure, you get to decide how you want to be treated. For many people, that in itself is important, especially if religious reasons are involved. But for every single person out there, this document relieves their family and friends from having to make this decision. Period.

Remember that if you can communicate at all, the doctors are listening to you and not your living will. Therefore, if the doctor can just ask you if you want a feeding tube or any type of life sustaining procedure, they will simply ask you. You can say yes or no. It's when the permanent coma or persistent vegetative state occurs that doctors must turn to the living will.

3. & 4. Medical Powers of Attorney and Financial Powers of Attorney (POAs)

A power of attorney (POA) is a document that allows you to name an individual, called an "agent," to act for you if you become incapacitated. **These are vital to keeping your family out of the court system if you are in an accident.** A will protects you and your family after you pass; POAs protect you while you are still alive.

If you don't have POAs and a doctor determines that you are incapable of making your own decisions—either due to being in a coma or otherwise becoming mentally incapacitated—you will end up having a guardian and conservator appointed by the court to make your medical and financial decisions. Guardianship and conservatorship hearings are expensive and can result in your having a stranger in charge of your life decisions. Not only does this person not know you, but also, you have to pay him or her an hourly rate to make your decisions. The hearing itself is expensive enough, but adding an hourly rate for a professional guardian and a professional conservator eats up your assets very quickly. The result is that people in this situation leave much less behind for their family to inherit, if anything at all.

Putting the proper POAs in place saves your family the headache and heartache of working with a court-appointed professional; it also saves money and avoids the stress of court. You get to name your agent, and your agent can be anyone you want. Do not let the name fool you; just because it is called a "power of attorney" does not mean you need to appoint an actual attorney. You can name a friend, family member, or professional fiduciary to this role. There are advantages to each. A lawyer should be consulted to make sure the best possible people fill these roles.

Medical Power of Attorney

A medical POA allows you to name an individual to make your medical decisions should you become incapacitated. Your medical agent can do the following:

- Talk to doctors
- Grant medical releases
- Access your medical records

- Help with long-term-care decisions

- Organize hospice care and more

A medical POA is in charge of any medical issue that arises while you are incapacitated. The financial savings associated with naming a medical POA in advance of an accident include avoiding enormous court costs and the associated attorney fees, and having to pay a professional fiduciary to make these decisions for the rest of your life.

Financial Power of Attorney

Like a medical POA, a financial POA allows you to name an agent to act for you. This agent makes all choices regarding paying your bills and managing your finances. A financial agent can do the following:

- Access your bank accounts

- Pay your bills

- Control and transfer your assets

- Complete gifts to others on your behalf

- Sign documents for you

A financial power of attorney cannot override your decisions while you still have capacity to act. They must act in your best interests at all times, and perform their duties as if they were you.

Having access to someone's assets is a tremendous amount of power, so putting the right person in charge is

critical. The role is essential to make sure that everything stays current while you recover. Then, if you regain capacity, your bills will be paid and your life can begin to return to normal.

You now have a deeper knowledge of the four main estate-planning documents that make up a solid estate plan. These are not *all* the documents that make a full plan; they are just the ones you will run into most often. Now that you have a firm grasp of these core elements, let's look at some of those other documents that round out a thorough estate plan.

Deeper Explanations of Other Documents You May Have Heard Of

Let's talk about some of the other documents you may be wondering about:

1. Health Insurance Portability and Accountability Act (HIPAA) Release

2. Personal Property Memorandum

3. Declaration of Final Remains Document

4. Revocable Living Trust

5. Irrevocable Trust

6. Delegation of Parental Rights

Health Insurance Portability and Accountability Act (HIPAA) Release

A Health Insurance Portability and Accountability Act release, or HIPAA release, is a document that states who is entitled to access your medical records. For most people, listing your medical power of attorney and any backups to your medical POA is the status quo. However, it could also be wise to list your financial POA and backups, as well as your personal representative, in case they need access to your medical records for any reason.

This document also has a more practical purpose. Anyone you list on this document will be allowed to be in the same room as your medical power of attorney and your doctor when they are discussing your diagnosis and any plans for surgery or recovery. **This means if you want people to have firsthand knowledge from the doctor about what is going on with your health, you should list them on your HIPAA release.** That way, your medical POA is not weighed down with the responsibility of trying to translate into plain English what a doctor said. All parties will hear it for themselves and be able to ask any questions they have.

If you do not wish for anyone but your power of attorney to be present with your doctor, then that is completely fine as well. In that case, just list your medical POA. In the end, the point of the document is to make your medical POA's life easier and ensure they have access to everything they need.

Personal Property Memorandum (PPM)

Do you have special items or family heirlooms you would like to pass on to specific people, like your children? If so, the Personal Property Memorandum (PPM), is the perfect place to do so. This is a two-column, one-page document. In the left column, you list what assets you have that you want to transfer on your death. In the right column, you list which people you want to receive those assets. It's that simple.

There are a few rules to follow in order to make this document binding. First, everything has to be in your handwriting. If someone else fills out the document, it won't be a valid transfer of property on your death. There is an exception to this rule if it is a fiduciary, like your power of attorney, filling the document out on your behalf. However, let's stick with the assumption that it's safest if you fill it out yourself.

Second, the document must be signed and dated by you. This one is critical. While you do not need any notaries, witnesses, or attorneys involved, you still have to sign and date it or it won't work to transfer property.

Third, you have to list personal property and *only* personal property. This document cannot and will not transfer title to real estate like land or your house. It can transfer titles to cars and mobile homes, however. Another thing people often try to transfer with these documents is cold, hard cash. This won't work here. If you want to leave land, houses, or cash, those items must be specifically listed in a will.

There are some other considerations that go into having a valid PPM, and it is always helpful to ask an attorney prior to filling it out.

The PPM has made things a lot simpler. It used to be that every time grandma wanted to update who got her silverware or wedding ring, lawyers had to draft an entirely new will (or an update called a "codicil") and then have an entirely new will-signing appointment. This was very time-consuming and not very cost-effective for grandma. With the addition of the PPM, now all grandma has to do is fill out a new PPM. That's it. She doesn't need a notary. She doesn't need any witnesses. And most importantly, she doesn't need to pay a lawyer to do anything.

Declaration of Final Remains Document

The Declaration of Final Remains Document goes by many names. By no means is it a set form. All attorneys who have this document (not all do) most likely have their own versions that they have customized over the years. **I mentioned earlier my belief that the living will is the most important document estate planners create for individuals. This document is the second most important.** It allows you to decide four main things:

1. Do you want to be buried?
2. Do you want to be cremated?
3. Do you want to have a funeral?
4. Do you prefer a memorial service?

After you decide those four main issues, this document then goes into detail on questions that could arise within those issues. **Like the living will, this document takes these**

stressful and often previously undiscussed decisions away from everyone else. It allows you to make these choices while you have the capacity to do so. If you have ever tried to grieve while also trying to decide if your loved one wanted a church ceremony, where they wanted to be buried, if they wanted flowers, what scripture they wanted read, and a whole slew of other decisions, you know it's tough. If you haven't had to do that, consider yourself lucky.

This document allows your family and loved ones to grieve properly without having to worry if they are doing things right by you.

My clients receive a fifteen-page Declaration of Final Remains Document. They get a chance to review things on their own and come up with answers. Then I help them through any tough choices and provide recommendations based on experience. The beauty of this document is that if something really matters to you, you get to make your choices known. If something doesn't matter to you, you can simply write "not applicable," "N/A," or "I don't care," and the rest of the document is still valid. Your family will know what you would have wanted. None of us want our families to have to guess on whether or not they did it right.

Revocable Living Trust (RLT)

Trusts come in all shapes and sizes. To cover every type of trust on the planet, we would be here for a very long time.

So we'll stick to the basics. When most people hear of a trust, it's a Revocable Living Trust, or RLT. This type of trust is created while you are alive and acts much like a will, but with the advantage of possibly avoiding probate.

Let's slow down a bit and remind ourselves of what exactly a trust is: a large stack of papers that allows an individual to declare where they want their things to go when they pass away. The person creating the trust is called the **trustor or settlor**. This person assigns an individual to be in charge of the trust. That person is the **trustee**. The trustor/settlor decides who will eventually get the property that is placed in trust. Those people are the **beneficiaries**.

Let's do a quick recap before moving on:

- **Trustor/Settlor:** person who creates the trust (you)
- **Trustee:** person in charge of the trust property (this can also be you, but you want to name successors as well)
- **Beneficiary:** person who will receive the trust property
- **Trust:** the vehicle that holds the property of the trustor/settlor that will eventually be distributed to the beneficiaries (usually a bank account)

Now let's look at **how the trust relationship works and how it can possibly avoid probate**, while a will normally cannot. First, think of a trust as its own entity, like a corporation. A RLT can have its own tax identification number or employer identification number (also known as an EIN), and it will potentially have to file income taxes if it makes enough money and you are not reporting the income on your own return. Many people just use their own Social Security number for the trust and report income how they normally would on their own tax return, rather than having the trust file its own taxes.

You can think of the trustee as the CEO of that corporation. The trustee is the decision maker who has the final say in what happens with the trust property. One final and critical thing to understand about a trust: **it can only control the property that it owns. This means you have to *fund*, or retitle, all of your assets into the trust—or the trust fails.**

Improper trust funding is the number one reason trusts fail. Let's look at an example to highlight the risks:

John Doe creates a RLT instead of a will because he wants his family to avoid the probate process. John does an excellent job of funding his trust by retitling his house, cars, and all personal property into the trust. However, John eventually moves and buys a new house in his own name years after forming the RLT. He forgets to purchase the home in the name of the trust and does not properly fund it to the trust before he passes away. Now what happens? Does the trust fail completely? Not exactly.

As far as the property the trust already owns, like the cars and personal property, all of that does pass according to the terms of the trust and will successfully avoid probate. However, the house was not funded (retitled) to the RLT, so it will now have to go through probate. Plus, since John had *only* a trust and *not* a complete will, **the house will go through probate as if no estate plan existed at all**. This ends up costing John Doe and his family twice as much in the long run, because he now has a probate *and* a problematic trust administration to handle.

This situation is very common with trusts—but can be avoided. All trust-based plans should contain a small will, called a **pour-over will**, that states that if anything is not properly funded into the trust before John dies, then ownership of that property is transferred into the trust at death. However, that does *not* stop the property from going through probate. It will eventually get it into the trust, but you still have to pay for the probate process and the trust administration separately.

This is why trusts *possibly* avoid probate. The trust can only control what it owns and can only make the property it owns avoid probate. Everything else will go through the probate process.

When do you need a trust then, you ask? There are many reasons but here are three main ones:

1. **You own property in multiple states**. This one is important because if you own property in Colorado, Florida, and California (or any other state), you will

have to go through a probate in all three states. **If you own property in a state, and that property is not retitled into a trust, then you have to go through probate in that state.** It can be very costly to go through multiple probates; you have to hire lawyers in all states and get court approval in all states. A trust pulls all of that property into your home state and avoids probate everywhere (assuming it is properly funded).

2. **You have a complex family situation.** The most common complex family situation is a Brady Bunch one. If John Doe has children from his first marriage and marries Jane, who also has children from a prior marriage, a trust may be useful in splitting assets properly. In these situations, spouses often want to make sure their children receive their fair share of assets, instead of the spouse taking everything and possibly disinheriting the other children. It's not that the other spouse would do this intentionally (though he or she might), but the law works in such a way that the children get the short end of the stick if no estate plan is in place.

Another common complex family situation involves protecting children from themselves. If children suffer from certain diseases; have mental illnesses; are receiving welfare; are on Medicaid; or if they have drug, alcohol, or gambling problems, a trust can help. **This is because a trust lets you decide when and how your children**

will receive money. It can be over the course of their lives and only for housing, or it can be for educational expenses and only if they get good grades. You decide how you want the money to be dished out.

If your children are eventually on any type of government benefit, it is possible that your inheritance could disqualify them from receiving those benefits. Medicaid is the most common culprit here. Being disqualified from Medicaid can be a large thorn in anyone's side. The disqualified person is forced to engage in what is called a "spend down." This means they essentially have to waste their inheritance immediately to avoid any Medicaid penalties. While spend downs are more complicated than that, the point here is that a trust can minimize, if not completely eliminate, this problem.

3. **You have tons of money.** This one isn't a joke. There is such a thing as an estate tax. Some states have their own estate tax levels to worry about, but not all of them (Colorado does not). The federal government also has an estate tax that you must consider, but the amount is very high: $5,490,000 per person passing in 2017 and 11.18 million dollars per person passing in 2018. That means that if you passed away in Colorado in 2017 as a single person with less than $5,490,000 (or $10,980,000 as a married couple) you didn't have to pay any estate taxes. In 2018, that number has doubled

to over 22 million dollars for a married couple. Most people don't have to worry about this number because it keeps growing each year. If you are approaching this number, however, trusts can give you creative options for avoiding the estate tax.

If you fall into any of these three categories, it's a good idea to at least discuss a trust. However, it does not mean that you absolutely need one. There are plenty of other options and tools that can be used with a will-based plan to save you money, time, and the headache involved with trust administration, trust funding, and all the other goodies that come with trusts. **If someone is telling you that you absolutely need a trust because will-based plans just can't give you the protections you need, I strongly recommend a second opinion.** That is not to say the first opinion is wrong. Trusts can play a very important role in many plans, but not everyone needs one.

Irrevocable Trust

Irrevocable trusts are a much different animal than most other documents we have talked about because, as their name implies, you can't revoke them. Every other document can be torn up, thrown out, set on fire, or otherwise destroyed to revoke it. Here, you can't do that. That fact alone makes irrevocable trusts dangerous in some situations, but they can also be incredibly helpful if used correctly. **If there was one place I could advise people, "Please never do this document on your own," this would be that place.**

There are many types of trusts that can be irrevocable, and I could write an entire book just dedicated to those types of trusts, but here, I will focus on the two main ones:

1. *Family Trust and Marital Trust Plans*

    Many people will want to create a Family Trust to provide certainty that nothing can be revoked and their children won't be disinherited. Their intent is that, when one spouse passes away, the plan then becomes irrevocable so as to provide for the remaining spouse for life *and* make sure their children do not get disinherited. This type of trust makes it so the surviving spouse cannot change the plan later, or remarry and unintentionally mess things up. Without getting too technical, the basics of this plan say that upon the first spouse's death, most assets will be funneled into the Family Trust first, up to the estate tax exemption amount of $11,180,000 in 2018. This money can be used to benefit the surviving spouse and the children until the surviving spouse passes away. At that point, the money transfers to the children, or however the Family Trust directs.

    The remaining money above $11,180,000 is funneled into a Marital Trust, sometimes referred to as a Qualified Terminable Interest Property trust, or QTIP trust. This money benefits the surviving spouse for life and then transfers per the terms of the QTIP trust, which is usually to the children. The point of this plan is to avoid probate, get money to the intended beneficiaries, and take advantage of the full estate tax exemption amount (to be discussed in more detail later).

2. *Irrevocable Life Insurance Trusts*

   Known as ILITs (pronounced "eye-lits"), these are also used to transfer money to intended beneficiaries and take advantage of the estate tax exemption amount. When you have an ILIT, you have created a trust that will purchase insurance policies on your life. The trust usually owns the policies, and your children, or whomever you name, can be the beneficiaries. Since you do not own the policy itself, the value of the policy is not included in your estate and you are not taxed on that amount when you pass away. The catch is that you can't be the trustee of this trust if you want to get the tax advantages. If you have any sign of ownership of the policies, they will be included in your estate.

   For most people, these trusts are a thing of the past. Since the estate tax exemption amount is so high, most people do not have to worry about paying estate taxes anymore. It is good to be aware of them, however. If the estate tax should ever be lowered in the future, these trusts will play a more important role again.

Delegation of Parental Rights (also known as Delegation of Parental Authority)

For parents who are having their children stay with family or friends for an extended period of time, a Delegation of Parental Rights (DPR) may come in handy. This document simply allows you to state that the individual you name in the document has the same parental decision-making capabilities that you have. In no way are you forfeiting your parental rights here. You are still the parent. (The only way to forfeit your parental rights is through the family courts, and that is not what a delegation does.) If you need someone to act as a parent for an extended period of time—dealing with school, housing, food, and all the other needs a child has—then a DPR may be for you.

Another common need for this document can arise if one spouse passes away and the surviving spouse has no means to support him- or herself, let alone a child. In these unfortunate circumstances, it can be very beneficial to issue a DPR so that a loved one other than the surviving spouse may help raise the child with more ease.

These documents do have one catch in some states. The catch is that the time period in which the document is effective can be limited. In Colorado, for example, it's one year. If you want the delegation to extend for a longer period of time, you must issue a new document every year.

You now have a pretty good idea of the types of documents that combine to constitute a full estate plan. By using different combinations of all the legal tools you have learned about thus far, you can start to see how a complete plan will protect you and your family in all different types of situations. Next, let's cover deeds and how they impact estate planning.

Deeds – How Do They Impact Your Planning?

Deeds can play a critical role in any estate plan. They have also been known to be the fastest way to destroy a plan. **Do not attempt to draft a deed for any of your properties without first consulting a lawyer.** An estate attorney can advise you on the consequences the deed may have on your current strategy.

What exactly is a deed anyway? A deed is a piece of paper that allows you to legally transfer title of your real property, such as a house, land, or mineral rights. Depending on the deed, you are passing title while alive, immediately upon your death, or after you pass and the property goes through probate.

Most Common Deed Types

Warranty Deeds

A warranty deed is what a buyer receives when purchasing a new home. This deed states that the seller has clear title. This means that no one else on the planet is supposed to be able to come in and say that they have better title than you do after you purchase the property (which is nice if you expect to stay in your home and not get evicted by a stranger).

Warranty deeds are most commonly used to transfer title of a home or land from a seller to a new, third-party buyer.

Quitclaim Deeds

Quitclaim deeds also transfer title of property. However, a quitclaim deed *makes no guarantee* by the seller/transferor that they actually have clear and marketable title, which means that someone could later come in and claim that they have better title than you and actually own your house.

Quitclaim deeds are commonly used to quickly transfer property between spouses, and sometimes other family members. **This is a very dangerous practice with very serious ownership and tax consequences. It should NOT be completed without first consulting an attorney.**

Beneficiary Deeds

Beneficiary deeds are excellent estate-planning tools that can help you avoid probate and get your property where you want it to go after you pass away. They are not allowed in every state, however, and some states refer to them by different names. Colorado does allow them and they work very well, but they can have a few downsides.

One downside is that Medicaid will usually not cover you if you have a beneficiary deed recorded on your property (keep in mind that Medicaid is different than Medicare). This is because Medicaid is a welfare program that pays your bills for you with the assumption you have no assets to pay those bills yourself. Medicaid will want to be reimbursed if you have assets, like a home, that they can make a claim against later down the line. If you had a beneficiary deed recorded, it would escape Medicaid's claim, and they do not like that.

Another possible downside is encountered if you plan to move a lot or you own multiple properties. You need to record a beneficiary deed on each property you own to avoid probate. You also need to have a new beneficiary deed recorded on each house you move to or purchase in the future. If you don't plan to move much and don't own a lot of property, this is not an issue.

The upside of a beneficiary deed is that it transfers ownership of your property upon your death. This means that you retain all rights to your property while you're still alive, including being able to sell it, mortgage it, refinance it, and so on. If you draft a beneficiary deed to your children, for example, your children have absolutely no rights to the property until you pass away. This also means that your children's creditors can't come after your property either. You do not obtain the same result with a quitclaim deed. If you quitclaim your property to your kids, they immediately take ownership and can evict you, and their creditors can now have access to it in order to place liens on it.

Personal Representative Deeds

Personal representative deeds, or PR deeds, are used in the probate process. These deeds allow your estate to legally transfer title of any real property that you may have at your death. Depending on what type of probate you are in, a judge or probate registrar may sign off on the final accounting of your estate, thus approving the sale of your assets through this type of deed.

PR deeds do not come into play much during the planning process because they are the responsibility of your personal representative during probate.

What's All This I Hear About "Basis"? What Does It Have to Do with Deeds?

I tell my clients that one of the biggest and best gifts they leave their family when they pass away is called a **step-up in basis**, often shortened to "basis." Basis is what you paid for a piece of property. Let's say you bought your home for $300,000. Your basis in your home is now $300,000. If you later sell that house for $1,300,000, the IRS dings you with short- or long-term capital gains taxes for $1,000,000 in income. This means you have to pay a bunch of taxes on the million dollars you just made selling your house for an amount above your basis.

If you quitclaim or otherwise gift your house during your life to your child or another person, that person receives what the IRS calls a "carry-over basis." This means they get the same basis you had in the property—so, you guessed it: $300,000.

Here's where dying actually has some benefits. If you pass away and your child receives your property through a beneficiary deed or through your will in the probate process, that child gets the magical "step-up in basis" instead of a "carry-over basis." Using the example above, your child now has a basis in your house of $1,300,000. This means that your child could turn around and sell the home the next day for $1,300,000 and pay $0 in taxes to the IRS. This is why basis is so important. Knowledge of it can potentially save your loved ones tens of thousands to hundreds of thousands of dollars.

The scary part about basis is that it is very easy to destroy by gifting property during your life, rather than after you pass away. Since the IRS doesn't go around explaining basis to people, many individuals have no idea it is something that can be passed along. You give a better basis to your family if you pass away rather than gifting them property during life. Different situations can call for different actions, however, so it's always best to get advice before taking action.

Other Estate-Planning Considerations

Many people go into estate-planning meetings saying two very common things. First, "I don't have much of an estate," and second, "My situation is pretty straightforward and not complicated."

When completing your estate plan, your lawyer should instruct you to examine *all of your assets*. It should be known that *every person has an estate* and *every situation has its own unique complications*. If you own anything, you have an estate. If you have children, you have a very important estate consisting of living beings! Debt must be managed correctly in a plan because it is part of your estate too. Unfortunately, most debt doesn't die with you. It's both the smart and kind choice to address debt in your plan and not leave it to your loved ones to deal with once you are gone.

Because every situation has its own complications, it is critical for you and your lawyer to look at your entire asset portfolio. How you own what you own plays a huge role in how things are distributed once you pass away. Below, we will get into two main areas that can override your will and cause serious havoc if not properly planned for.

Beneficiary-Designated Assets

When completing your estate plan, it is critical to analyze how your beneficiary-designated assets are set up. Beneficiary-designated assets consist of every single thing you own that has a beneficiary designation or a payable-on-death (POD) designation. This can include:

- Life insurance policies
- IRAs
- 401(k)s
- Bank accounts and more

Why are these assets so important to analyze? Because whomever you name as your beneficiary will receive that property regardless of what your will says. **Beneficiary-designated assets *override* your will.** This is critical to understand, so let me lay out an example:

John Doe recently had children and wants them to inherit everything he has equally. Prior to having kids, John Doe had a really good family friend, Jake Friend, who helped him pay his way through college, so John Doe took out a $500,000 life insurance policy and listed Jake Friend as the beneficiary on that policy in hopes that if something happened to John, Jake could recover his money. However, over the years, John was able to pay Jake off completely. So, being the wise man John is, he drafted a will stating that his children should inherit everything, including his life insurance policy. The next day, John promptly keeled over.

Do John's kids get the life insurance policy or does Jake Friend? The answer is that Jake Friend gets the money; the kids are left without a penny of it. This is because beneficiary designated assets are a separate contract with a business, and under the law, that contract wins out over a will. Are there exceptions? Yes, but very few and you should never rely on them.

The bottom line is that you need to double check all your beneficiary designated assets to make sure everything lines up with your estate plan. Your lawyer should be able to tell you exactly how your beneficiaries should be listed on all of your assets so that you don't run into the problem that John Doe faced.

Avoiding Probate with Beneficiary-Designated Assets

I will not get into the pros and cons of avoiding probate yet, but what you should know is that by properly completing your beneficiary designations on your assets, you *will* ensure that those assets avoid probate. This means your beneficiaries can receive your property immediately on your passing, rather than possibly waiting six months or more for the probate to end.

That means beneficiary-designated assets make it possible to completely avoid probate *without a trust*. It takes some serious planning, but it is possible to avoid probate *with a will-based plan*.

Joint Ownership Versus Tenancy in Common

How you own your real property (houses and land) can also greatly impact how your things will be distributed once you pass away. If you own your home as a joint tenant with your spouse, then when you pass away, your house will automatically go to your spouse without the need for probate. If you own that same home as a tenant in common, your half of the house will have to go through probate before it passes to your spouse.

Here's an example of how this can be an enormous hassle:

John Doe is on his second marriage. His wife, Jane, is also on her second marriage. Both John and Jane have children from their prior relationships, and neither has adopted each other's children. When John and Jane bought their current house, they titled their home as tenants in common. The next day, John passed away. Who owns the home now? Unfortunately, Jane now owns 50% of the house and John's children own the other 50% in equal parts. That means they could force Jane out of her home by selling the property. It also means that if Jane wanted to refinance or sell her own home, she would need the approval of John's three children. This result can be changed in a will, but John's 50% will always have to go through probate, causing a delay in time for the title to properly pass. Not a very ideal situation.

Now let's say that John and Jane title the house as joint tenants when they first purchased it. When John passes away, the house will pass to Jane regardless of what John's will says. Nothing will pass through probate. (There are a few things that need to be done to properly transfer legal title to Jane, but they are small and take almost no time.)

It's important to note here that if John had wanted his three children to share in the proceeds of the house or have an ownership interest, they will receive nothing because joint tenancy overrides John's will (in the same way that beneficiary-designated assets override his will).

When you own something as joint tenants, both parties own 100% of the property at the same time, meaning the property passes to the joint owner immediately upon death without regard to what your will says. If you own something as tenants in common, you own only your share of the property (50% if there are two people), and your share must pass through your will before moving on to the rightful owners.

The other tenants in common do not have any right to your share unless you give it to them.

I can't stress enough how important *proper* ownership of your assets can be to your plan. Double-checking *how* you own things is critical to how your assets will eventually pass. A complete estate plan includes not only the documents, but also a professional review of your entire big picture.

Taxes

Ah yes, death and taxes. There are four main types of taxes we need to plan for with a proper estate plan. Everyone has encountered the first one: income tax. There are also three lesser-known taxes: the estate tax, the gift tax, and the generation-skipping transfer tax. Let's break down each one:

1. **Income Tax:** This is the tax the federal government and state governments charge on the income you bring home from your salary and a lot of other types of increases in wealth you receive throughout the year. For the purposes of estate planning, income tax is important to understand fully for a few reasons. First, different individuals have different tax rates, so it may be possible to transfer different types of income to individuals in lower tax brackets, thus saving you money on taxes in the long run. And second, certain types of assets you leave at death *can still have income tax consequences* for the beneficiaries. One example is

an IRA, or Individual Retirement Account. Consulting a lawyer or accountant about these tax implications is very important.

2. **Estate Tax:** The estate tax, sometimes called the death tax, is what the IRS collects if your estate exceeds the estate tax exemption amount when you pass away. For an individual, this amount was $5,490,000 in 2017 and $11,180,000 in 2018 (or double for married couples). Therefore, not many people are impacted by this tax; most of us pass away with well under the estate tax amount and do not have to pay any estate tax whatsoever. If you are above this amount, however, and do not plan for it, you could end up leaving half of your estate to the government. It's worth chatting about.

   One other key thing to note about the estate tax is that different states can have their own estate tax separate from the federal amount. Colorado currently has no estate tax, no inheritance tax, or anything similar. This doesn't mean you don't have to worry about the federal estate tax. You do; there is just no added state penalty. If you live outside of Colorado, you may have a much lower number to deal with. Minnesota, for example, had an estate tax exemption amount just over $2,000,000 in 2017, much lower than the federal limit. Planning in these types of states becomes much more important.

3. **Gift Tax:** The IRS also taxes large gifts. If you are giving more than $15,000 in 2018 to any one person throughout the calendar year, you are supposed to report that gift to the IRS and possibly pay tax on it. I won't get into the nitty gritty of when you actually pay tax because that can be very dependent on individual facts and circumstances. For our purposes, just know that anything under $15,000 in 2018 (that number is likely to stay the same or increase in following years) means you are in the clear and don't have to pay taxes on those gifts. What exactly is a gift? You give someone something, like cash, and receive nothing in return. If you want the drawn out legal definition, it is "giving something out of a detached and disinterested generosity involving affection, respect, admiration, charity, or like impulses."

   Gifting can be a very useful strategy in many estate plans. You can get your assets to your family, friends, or whoever else you want while you are still alive. If you have a large estate, you can start planning to avoid estate taxes by gifting throughout your life.

   It is important to note that the gift tax can hurt you. The most common example is when parents decide to retitle their house into their children's names, essentially gifting it to them. Many people believe this will get their property to their children, avoid taxes, and protect the asset from Medicaid. That assumption is wrong. First, retitling a house is a very large gift to your children that the IRS wants to know about. Second, Medicaid *can* claw back these types of transfers, especially if done fraudulently. **Never transfer title of your home without first talking to an attorney who is skilled in this area of law.**

4. **Generation-Skipping Transfer (GST) Tax:** The GST tax comes into play for those who want to transfer assets to their grandchildren or great-grandchildren. This tax assesses a tax on transfers, whether through a will or by gift while you are alive, to those who are more than one generation below you. This means if you "skip" your children and leave something directly to your grandchildren, there is a tax imposed. However, for most people, this tax doesn't apply because the threshold is the same as the estate tax: anything below $11,180,000 in 2018 you can use to "skip" without paying any taxes.

It's very important to analyze your full estate, including all policies, retirement plans, and bank accounts to make sure everything lines up. If completed correctly, it can avoid a lot a heartache and expenses down the line.

To Avoid Probate, or Not to Avoid Probate: That Is the Question.

Avoiding probate is something that many people hear about and are often determined to accomplish without really understanding why. I explained earlier in this book how a will-based plan sets you on a course to go through probate when you pass away, while if you draft and properly fund a trust, you and your family can avoid probate. In this chapter, we talk about whether avoiding probate is necessary because **there *are* advantages to going through probate**.

As a brief refresher, probate is the court-guided process by which legal title to your property is properly transferred. In more general terms, it is the way for the state to ensure that title to your stuff passes to the right people. With that in mind, let's understand why people wanted to start avoiding this process in the first place.

In the past, the laws surrounding probate were very different from what they are today. Probate used to take a year or longer to complete; the process was time-consuming and required court appearances. To make matters even worse, probate was very expensive. Attorneys used to charge a percentage of your estate (they still can in some states) and court fees added up quickly.

Today, laws have changed to make probate much more efficient. Colorado's laws have changed in ways that make it one of the easier states in which to complete the process. Many other states are changing to similar, more efficient laws. This is good news for many people, as probate is becoming simpler and less costly. Today, most attorneys will charge an hourly rate—if an attorney is needed at all. **For many estates, probate can be completed *without* the need for a lawyer's services and *without* having to appear in court at all.** Most probates are handled informally; there is much less court involvement and most communication is conducted through the mail, meaning you don't ever have to go to the courthouse.

This is not true for all probate matters. If there are fights, or litigation needs to happen, probate can be very time-consuming and costly. However, even if you try to avoid probate with a trust, fights can still arise. Even with a trust, similar costs will come into play if fights break out necessitating litigation.

Avoiding Probate – Pros and Cons

Avoiding probate means you meet the requirements so that your property does not have to go through the court system after you pass. There are three different ways to avoid probate: One, you drafted a trust and properly funded it, meaning you don't actually *own* anything anymore, so probate isn't necessary. Two, you properly lined up your beneficiary-designated assets and had a well-written, will-based estate plan, making it possible to avoid probate. Or three, you owned less than $66,000 in your name alone, with no real estate, thereby meeting the Small Estate laws in Colorado, meaning you don't need a probate. (Each state is different when it comes to this Small Estate amount.)

The Pros of Avoiding Probate:

1. **Saving time.** If no one is fighting and your plan has successfully avoided probate, your family members will receive the property you want them to receive immediately in most cases. This can save six months or more of their time.

2. **Saving money in the long run.** Avoiding probate usually costs a good amount more up front, with the goal of saving money in the future. If court and lawyers' fees can be avoided down the line, this does pay off.

3. **Avoiding lawyers.** This one is always a bonus! If you aren't going through probate and no one is fighting, then no lawyer needs to be involved.

4. **Avoiding stress.** Some probates can be very stressful, although that stress will likely exist with or without a probate. If people are fighting, they likely would have been fighting outside of probate. Fights, in the end, will usually wind up in court whether or not probate was initially avoided.

5. **Maintaining privacy.** The probate process is a public one. A notice has to be published in a local newspaper letting creditors know that the person has passed. Further, anyone can ask the court to see the will and the related court documents. This means almost anyone can find out what is going on with your most personal matters after you pass. Avoiding probate keeps things more private, since only the people named on the assets or in the trust have access to this information.

The Cons of Avoiding Probate:

1. **Missing the creditor cutoff period.** One giant benefit of going through probate is that you and your family get what is called a "creditor cutoff period." Once probate is initiated and a notice to creditors is published in the newspaper, creditors have a four-month period (in Colorado) to file a claim against the estate. If they fail to file a claim during this time period, they are barred from ever filing a claim. This means that the debt is wiped out completely; no one will ever have to pay it. If you avoid probate, you do not get the advantage

of this cutoff period, and creditors could technically submit a claim much further down the road. If your heirs have already spent their inheritance, the personal representative could be held personally responsible for the debt. Therefore, missing this period is a large con.

2. **Not obtaining court approval.** If you avoid probate, you do not get a judge to sign off on anything that anyone has done regarding the transfer of your assets. Court approval can mean a lot to the people who are in charge of transferring your assets, as it will relieve them of any liability down the road.

3. **Lacking supervision.** Going through probate gives you the advantage of having a judge or probate registrar in the background making sure the proper steps are taken, even if your personal representative never steps foot inside a courtroom. Avoiding probate means there is no supervision, which has led to criminal activity and mismanagement of funds.

4. **Increasing cost to you now to hopefully avoid cost down the road.** Many plans that are put in place to avoid probate are much more costly than plans that do not avoid probate. Sometimes they can be two to three times more expensive. This is a factor you will have to weigh when deciding what is right for you.

5. **Increasing uncertainty surrounding future purchases.** If you have everything funded into your trust today, or

your beneficiaries are all set up correctly now, you must make sure that if you sell property, buy new property, or change beneficiary assets, you retitle the new items so that they are titled properly. This does not mean you have to draft a new trust each time you buy property, but it does mean you have to remember to buy property in the name of the trust, or the trust will become useless. If you do not buy property in the name of the trust, then you *will* end up in a probate *and* have a somewhat-failed trust administration to deal with, costing you and your family more up front and in the long run.

There are some serious advantages and disadvantages to consider when deciding whether or not to have your estate go through probate. If you do go through probate, your family gets the advantage of a strict time limit that creditors have to make claims. Once this time period ends, no creditor can ever come back and say that your family owes them money. You do not get this cutoff period if you avoid probate. Further, going through probate means that your personal representative has the assurance that a judge has approved of his or her actions taken during the probate process. This way, no one can come back and say that the PR messed things up; your PR will be able to sleep easier knowing there isn't a lawsuit lingering off in the distance. You will be comforted knowing that there will be supervision of that which needs to happen, if that is something you were worried about in the first place.

Avoiding probate also has its own significant advantages if you want privacy, speed, and an opportunity to have a little more control over assets after you pass.

Whether or not to avoid probate isn't usually as complicated a decision as it once was. Is it nice to avoid probate in many cases? Yes. Does it save your family that much time and effort? Sometimes yes and sometimes no. My typical advice for clients is that avoiding probate is not a necessity. If it can be accomplished simply, then by all means, go for it. If it cannot, then there isn't much to worry about, as the laws have changed in ways to make the process fairly simple.

How to Prepare for Your Consultation with an Estate-Planning Lawyer

Now that you have an understanding of the different documents involved in estate planning, it's time to get ready to chat with an attorney. Preparing for your initial consultation with an estate planner is not as hard as it may seem. By reading this book you are already more prepared than most people. Really, it is up to the lawyer to instruct you on what to bring and what information he or she needs. However, here are some basics to help you feel more comfortable heading into the process:

What to Bring

When meeting with me, I tell clients that the main thing they need to bring is themselves. I also like to see any old estate-planning documents that have been completed—whether they were handwritten, done online, or drafted by a previous attorney. This way, I can get the full picture of what we are dealing with.

Another important thing to bring is any divorce decree or other court orders that have been issued for you. These are important because they may require that property pass to certain people, and a failure to follow those orders can result in jail time, huge fines, or both.

The last thing I like people to bring is a general knowledge of what their assets are and who their beneficiaries are on certain policies, like life insurance. That helps paint a complete picture and gives your lawyer a good base for being able to make sound recommendations for your plan.

What Questions to Ask Your Lawyer

One question everyone wants to know the answer to is, "How much is this going to cost me?" Costs vary greatly, and you should not be looking only for the cheapest option. As far as estate plans go, not every lawyer is as experienced as the next. That being said, there usually isn't a need to spend tens of thousands of dollars on a plan. I have seen lawyers charge this much for a plan that probably should have cost just a few thousand. **The important thing to do when pricing attorneys is talk to multiple lawyers and find out which one you feel most comfortable with.** If your plan is done right, you are going to be spending a good amount of time with this person, getting to know each other fairly well, and sharing some very personal information with him or her. The bottom line is that you should *like* your attorney.

As far as other cost-related questions go, make sure to ask the following:

- *Do you charge an hourly rate or a flat fee?* Some attorneys will charge an hourly rate based on the amount of time they put into the documents and meetings with you. This usually means you are getting billed for phone calls and emails as well. If you aren't careful, your costs could skyrocket. Other attorneys, myself included, will charge a flat fee based on the plan you choose; calls/emails and all other forms of communication are included. That is not to say one is better than the other; it is just something to be aware of.

- *Do you offer estate-planning packages?* In order to save people time and money, certain attorneys will package sets of documents together and charge a flat fee for the package. Other attorneys will put your plan together piecemeal depending on what you want. **In my opinion, an estate-planning professional should be guiding you on what documents you need for your specific situation.** After all, he or she the professional, and it is what you are paying him or her to do.

- *Are there different rates for different people at the firm?* Some attorneys will have associates or paralegals that do the actual drafting of your plan. If this is the case, those people should usually get billed out at a lower rate.

- *Are phone calls and email communications extra?* This is very good question to ask up front to avoid conflicts with your bill down the road. This is a huge area of unrest between clients and lawyers at the end of representation if it is not first brought up, answered, and understood in the beginning. It is my take that phone calls and emails should be free (up to a point) because I want you calling with your questions instead of trying to figure things out on your own and possibly making a mistake that could jeopardize your plan.

Once you understand how much you will be charged, you'll want to know what is included in that price. Questions that help at this stage include the following:

- *What documents will I receive?* Are you just getting a will, or are you getting a full plan with powers of attorney, a living will, a HIPAA release, and more? A full plan will help prepare for anything that happens down the road, while just receiving one or two documents will leave many holes in your estate.

- *Will my spouse and I receive separate documents?* Some attorneys will draft joint wills (not recommended) and others will do completely separate plans for each spouse (recommended).

- *Are there any documents I will need to complete on my own?* There are certain documents that attorneys legally cannot draft for you. Two important ones include the Medical Orders for Scope of Treatment (MOST) form and the Do Not Resuscitate order. These must be completed with your doctor. Your attorney may also have homework that is critical for you to complete.

You will also want to ask some follow-up questions regarding what happens after your plan is complete:

- *Are there any steps I will need to complete on my own?* Steps you may have to complete on your own could include funding of trusts, unfunding of trusts, retitling assets, and renaming beneficiaries on certain policies or bank accounts.

- *How often should I have my plan reviewed?* Generally, it is wise to get your plan reviewed when certain life events occur. Marriages, divorces, additions to the family, a loss in the family, or purchasing a new home are red-flag events. Some attorneys will offer a free review if you have completed your plan with them.

- *Is a periodic review included in my current price, or is that extra?* As mentioned above, some attorneys offer free reviews and others do not.

- *With whom should I be communicating regarding my plan?* It is usually wise to let your financial advisor, insurance person, doctor, and other key people know the essential components of your strategy.

- *To whom do I need to supply information regarding my plan?* Depending on the complexity of your plan, other professionals may need to be involved. Be sure to find out if your lawyer wants you to get in touch with other people.

- *Which individual at the law firm should I reach out to if I have questions?* Sometimes lawyers charge for questions if you call them directly, but do not charge if an associate is called. I believe you should find an attorney you can have direct access to, but that is your decision.

- *Which members of my family need to be involved?* Depending on whom you choose as your power of attorney and other "power people," certain members of your family may need to receive copies of your plan.

What Questions to Ask Yourself

As important as it is to ask your attorney plenty of questions to make sure you are on the same page, it is equally important to prepare yourself. Some things to think about include the following:

- *What is going to happen when you check out?* Would you prefer to be buried or cremated? Do you want your family to have a funeral for you, or do you prefer a memorial service? Who is paying for all of this?

- *Where do you want your things to go when you pass away?* This question seems simple on its face, but a good lawyer will ask you tougher questions regarding what happens if the people you want to receive your things pass away before you do. Also, think about whether or not you are charitably inclined.

- *Who do you want caring for your minor children if you are gone?* This is an extremely important issue for parents with minor children. Appointing someone now will save you and your family heartache and loads of money down the road.

- *Who do you want managing your finances and talking to your doctors if you are out of commission for a short while?* If you are incapacitated due to an accident, you need people to take care of your obligations until you are better. These are your powers of attorney. Whom do you want in charge?

People to Speak with Beforehand

It is common for people to try to keep their estate plan private. This is fine where the general public is concerned; however, it is absolutely *not a good idea* when it comes to the people who are directly impacted by your planning. Not only can keeping things secret from your family, your powers of attorney, and your personal representative cause confusion, it can lead to fights and costly litigation down the road. **I tell every single one of my clients that while the documents I draft for them are important, the conversations behind the documents are even more critical to the success of the plan.**

So, with whom should you definitely make sure to discuss things? First up are your "power people":

We begin with the **guardian** you name if you have minor children. This person, or set of people, will be in charge of becoming the parents of your minor children should anything happen to you. Of course, this is not something with which you want to surprise them. It is important to note that anyone you name as a power person in your will has the option to decline the position. Have the conversation *before* you name your guardian so you know they are willing and able to support your kids if the unexpected should occur. You don't want to pass away and then have your children find out the guardians can't take them, so they are going to foster care instead.

The next people you should speak with are your **medical and financial powers of attorney**. These people will be in charge of all of your assets and talking to your doctors. They will have to make decisions about what surgeries you will have and how to spend your money. **Don't just *ask* them if they are willing to do this; have a *discussion* with them**

about it. They should know what you would actually prefer that they do, how you would want to be treated in certain medical situations, and what actions are OK and not OK to take with your money.

Next up is your **personal representative**. This is the person who is in charge of the probate process after you pass away. He or she will be locating your assets, valuing them, dealing with creditors, and making sure things pass according to your will. Of all the power people you have, this is the one who is in the most thankless position. If someone is going to get yelled at, it is going to be the personal representative. Even if there are no fights and everything goes as planned, being a personal representative is still a lot of work and a tough job to do while grieving. **Think hard about whom you want for this role and have a serious conversation about whether or not that individual would want this responsibility.** Your attorney should be available to help your personal representative if he or she needs it.

If you have named a **trustee** in your plan, this person should be consulted too. (A trustee is very similar to the personal representative, except he or she is in charge of your trust, not your will.)

It should go without saying that if you have **backups** to any of the above-mentioned people—and you *should* have backups—you need talk to them as well.

Now to the **beneficiaries** of your plan. These are the people you name to inherit your property. Whether or not you choose to discuss how much a person will be receiving is completely up to you. Your attorney can lend advice, but the decision is yours to make. In my opinion, I prefer to let people know *who* will be inheriting, but not necessarily *how much*. A worry a lot of clients have is that if individuals know they are going to inherit a large sum of money, it may dissuade them from pursuing certain careers. If you are disinheriting someone who would normally inherit from you, I do recommend having that conversation with everyone involved. It will greatly reduce the chances of a future "will contest" and help to keep your family out of costly litigation when you pass.

Another thing to note here is that your lawyer cannot, should not, and never can be a beneficiary in your plan. Do not draft him or her into your will. If he or she requests to be drafted into your will, then run for the hills. This is highly unethical and could get the attorney disbarred.

Finally, I believe it is critical to have a discussion surrounding your entire plan with **your family members**. Even if they are not listed anywhere in your documents, everyone should have a general idea of what you want to happen, where you want your things to go, and whom you want running the show. If everyone knows what is supposed to happen, no one can fight about it. I can't tell you how many times I have heard, "My children get along great; we don't have to worry about fights," and then have seen fights arise when mom and dad are gone. The bottom line is that death can bring out the worst in people. This is an unfortunate truth that many people refuse to believe until they see it for themselves. It's better to plan ahead now and nip it in the bud rather than wait and hope for the best.

What Happens After Your Consultation?

I can't speak to what every estate planner's process is after an initial consultation, but here's a breakdown of a fairly standard timeline:

Planning Meeting

The initial consultation is used to get to know each other, determine if you would work well together, and obtain some very basic information. The Planning Meeting is the next meeting in the process and where the actual details of your plan get hammered out. For this meeting, you will likely need to bring some homework that needs to be completed beforehand. Your attorney will provide that to you during the initial consultation.

At the Planning Meeting you will review any homework and have your questions answered. You will then dive into how you want your property to be distributed and to whom you want it to go. If you are married, the talk will involve an in-depth discussion on how things should pass upon the first spouse's death, and then again upon the second spouse's death. You must also begin a conversation on what happens if someone you want to inherit predeceases you. Would you want that person's children (your grandkids, for instance) to inherit? Or would you prefer someone else (like your surviving children) inherit instead?

You will also address issues involving charitable inclinations. Do you want to leave something to a charity? Is that going to provide you with a tax advantage? Do you have a church or other organization you care deeply about and want to leave in your will?

After you address all the property issues with your lawyer, you will move on to deciding whom you want your power people, or agents, to be. This means deciding on:

- A personal representative (formerly known as an executor)
- A guardian (if minor children are involved)
- A financial power of attorney
- A medical power of attorney
- A trustee
- Possibly others, depending on your plan

Once you get your power people nailed down, it is highly recommended that you designate backups for each position in case something happens to your primary agent. This helps your plan continue to work even if you never talk to another attorney again regarding updates.

Signing Meeting

After your Planning Meeting, the next step is for your lawyer to use all the information to draft your documents. You will then meet for a review and Signing Meeting. The first part (it may be two separate meetings) is to review your documents in person to ensure you fully understand everything that is in them and how they work. If any changes need to be made, that can easily take place at this time.

Once everything is understood and approved, it's time to make you official! Your lawyer will have two witnesses present, as well as a notary to watch you sign. These individuals are attesting to the fact that you have the capacity to sign your will and you *did,* in fact, sign it. This helps to minimize the chances of someone coming along in the future and contesting your will by saying you were incompetent at the time of signing, or it wasn't actually you who signed the document.

After you sign, the witnesses sign, and the notary places his or her seal on the documents, you are done. Congratulations; you now have a fully functioning estate plan! Your attorney should scan the documents and keep digital copies of the originals ***forever.*** The attorney may also be willing to make copies for your power people so you don't have to.

Family Meeting

The final meeting that I like to have for my clients is called a Family Meeting. At this meeting, I start off by giving the original documents back to the client, explaining the next steps involved, and answering any remaining questions the clients may have.

This meeting is also an opportunity for you to bring in your family and power people so they can hear straight from the estate planner what their roles are going forward. This affords them the opportunity to ask questions and receive the answers they need to do their jobs effectively. It is also a great chance to put a face with a name and make sure everyone in the family knows to whom they can reach out if they ever need help in an emergency.

You're All Done. What Now?

Completing your estate plan is a huge step toward having peace of mind and knowing that your hard-earned assets will go where you want. You know that your family will be properly protected in case of the unexpected. You also know that you won't be leaving a mess for them to clean up.

So, at this point, are you completely finished and never have to worry about anything regarding estate-planning ever again? I wish I could say yes, but there are still a few things to keep in mind.

Get Your Original Documents

Depending on your lawyer's policies, he or she may keep your original documents, or you may get them back. My recommendation is that you keep your original documents. This way, if that law firm goes out of business, the lawyer passes

YOU ONLY DIE ONCE

away, or any other unexpected event occurs, you know where your documents are at all times. Your lawyer should always have scanned copies of your originals, just in case.

It is also important for you to have your original documents in case a doctor, financial institution, or other professional requires that the originals be presented rather than a copy. For example, if there is an emergency at two o'clock in the morning, what happens if a doctor won't speak to your medical power of attorney without the original document? (Odds are that copies will suffice, but I've seen weirder things happen.) Your lawyer's office is likely not open at 2:00 a.m. Either way, it is your best bet to have your originals safely in your home.

Give Copies to the Correct People and Never Write on Them!

When I complete a plan for my clients, I make sure to print off enough copies of every document for all the power people we have named. This includes the medical power of attorney, financial power of attorney, personal representative, trustee, guardian, and all the backups to those positions.

If you are in an accident at an odd hour or need emergency assistance right away, it is much easier if your power people have *their own copies* ready to go rather than trying to hunt down where you put your originals. Most businesses and hospitals are fine with copies, so it makes perfect sense for your trusted power people to have those in their possession for easy access.

One recommendation I make is that you stamp the copies as "copies." This way, no one can start writing on the copies and claim that it was your original you wrote on with the intent to change who gets what (more on this shortly). Once again, keep the originals safe.

How Do I Keep My Documents Safe? Safe-Deposit Box?

Clients often tell me that they are headed to the bank after their will signing to put their documents in a safe-deposit box. I immediately instruct them on different options. While it is *sometimes* acceptable to put your will in a safe-deposit box, *I do not recommend keeping other documents with it.* This relates to the above example regarding your 2:00 a.m. accident. Banks are not usually open in emergency situations, and your power people need access to your documents at all hours in case something unexpected happens. If your documents are locked in a bank vault somewhere, they may be impossible to get when you need them most. This is also why it is so important that your power people have their own copies to store in their homes.

If you do go the route of a safe-deposit box for all your documents—to be clear, against my recommendations—then you should at least make sure that your personal representative and powers of attorney have access to the box. This will prevent problems down the line when your power people need access. It can be very difficult for people who aren't given official access to open your safe-deposit box both while you are alive and after you have passed.

Again, my advice here is **do not use a safe-deposit box for your original estate-planning documents**. Get a fireproof safe in your house instead and keep all of your documents together inside of it.

I am serious about this—the good ol' fireproof safe. They are relatively inexpensive for how convenient and important they are. **If you store your original documents all together in one place, your family won't have an issue deciphering what you wanted to happen in case of an emergency or after you are gone.** Everything will be together and your power people will be able to access all of your documents when necessary.

Of course, your chosen people must know how to get into your fireproof safe. This seems obvious, but it's a point worth emphasizing. Whether that means giving them an extra key or telling them the combination, make sure your power people know how to access your safe and what it contains.

Never Write on Your Documents!
Ask an Attorney If You Need Updates.

I cannot stress this enough: never write on your final estate-planning documents because it can potentially revoke your plan, whether you intend to or not. Look, you have spent time educating yourself on what planning you need and gone through the process of picking the right attorney to draft your plan. You don't want to accidentally make it all fall apart by writing on your documents.

The main thing people do unintentionally to revoke parts or all of their will (or any planning document) is to cross out names and addresses because people have moved or predeceased them. Sometimes people change their minds about who they want to inherit, and they falsely believe they can just cross a person out—and voilà—that person is written out of the plan. That is a myth. What happens in reality is that you have created a giant hole in your document that could revoke it or allow others to more easily challenge it in the future.

The easiest way to stop this problem is to *never write on your estate-planning documents*. I'll say it one more time for good measure: Never write on *any* of your estate-planning documents.

Common reasons for needing updates that lead people to write on their plans include:

- Buying a new home or changing addresses
- Changing your mind about whom you want serving as a power person
- Deciding to disinherit someone
- Deciding to leave something extra to someone who was not originally named in your will
- Having an individual predecease you
- Gaining a new member of the family (new baby, new grandchild, etc.)

If any of these life events happen to you, by all means have your plan revisited. But do not, under any circumstance, start making the changes yourself.

If you ever have a question regarding your plan or feel like you need to update it, call your lawyer. It's worth the time and energy. If your lawyer drafted your plan, odds are that he or she is willing to talk for a few minutes on whether or not changes even need to be made. While there may be a small fee for an update, it's well worth it to prevent your entire plan from being revoked.

Should I Just Do It Myself?

My honest recommendation for everyone is do not attempt to create an estate plan on your own. Having read this guide, you now understand how much more complex a full estate plan is compared to what people usually think when heading into the planning process.

I compare an estate plan to a Jenga tower. With a complete estate plan drafted by a knowledgeable lawyer, you have all the pieces of a full tower. Not only that, but the pieces are glued together and supported by iron beams on all sides. It is highly unlikely this tower will fall.

When you complete a plan by yourself, however, the chances of your missing necessary documents or drafting a document incorrectly increases exponentially. **Every document you leave out removes a few pieces from the Jenga tower,**

making it less stable and more susceptible to collapse. If you draft even one document wrong, it could be the gust of wind that topples the tower. When the tower falls, your plan fails completely. This means that your family is left in uncertainty and possibly disinherited.

I will go through the pros and cons of each side—on your own or with professional help—so you can make the decision for yourself.

The Pros

Cost Savings

The obvious pro of doing things on your own is the low cost up front. If you draft all your own documents, there is virtually no cost at all. If you use the services of an online document factory, you may pay a few hundred dollars for everything you think you need.

However, you will not usually get any advice included with the original fee. One area these online companies "get" people is by luring you in with a low-cost will, but then charging a lot more for all the additional documents and even more to speak with a representative, who may or may not be an attorney. Be careful with online companies. They sometimes hire individuals who have passed the bar exam but never practiced law. This allows the company to say they have employed "attorneys" to give you advice, while in reality, that "attorney" may have never actually drafted a will in his entire life.

No Lawyers

Another big pro for some people is that you don't have to deal with a lawyer if you complete your plan yourself. My response here is that you should be able to weed out the lawyers who aren't a good fit for you by interviewing many candidates. **Estate planning is a personal business in which relationships matter, and it should be an honor for your lawyer to help you out, not the other way around.**

Privacy

The final big pro for some individuals is keeping their matters completely private. If you do your own plan, there is no way for others to find out about it unless you tell them. This can be beneficial if a person feels that the decisions he or she is making would hurt others' feelings, aren't in the normal sphere of decisions, or just plain aren't anybody else's business. The downside to this is, if no one knows your plan, how will it ever be carried out? There is also no guarantee, of course, that you drafted the plan correctly.

The Cons

No Guarantees

The first big con to doing an estate plan without a lawyer is there are no guarantees your wishes will be carried out. When the right attorney drafts a plan, he or she can be confident in telling the client that *it will work exactly how it is drafted* until the day that person passes away and beyond (barring any acts of God or severe law changes).

I know this because I have seen my clients' documents go through the courts. They have been challenged, and they prevailed. I have also seen what happens when people don't have a plan, when people have partial plans, and when people have great plans that work. I know what missteps to avoid and how to properly plan for situations that can unexpectedly arise. Most estate-planning attorneys who have been in practice long enough can say the same thing. While no one can promise results based on prior cases, every ounce of experience helps.

It's Possible to Disinherit People Accidentally; It's Happened

When drafting your will, if you leave someone out accidentally, it may mean that they won't receive anything—even if you wanted them to. What is more important about this situation is that it leaves a big hole in your plan that has a high potential to cause litigation in the future. Litigation is extremely costly, time-consuming, and takes a significant toll on those involved. You want to avoid your family having to hire a lawyer later to litigate issues that could have been prevented today.

Another thing to think about regarding disinheriting people is the issue that arises when family members are born *after* you draft your will. That new child or grandchild may be cut out if changes to the will aren't made properly.

Creating Trusts on Your Own Can Cause You to Lose Control You Did Not Intend to Lose

Let's look at an example for this one. A personal-injury attorney decided to draft his own estate plan. Although he had never drafted a plan before, since he was a lawyer, he figured he could manage. Even with the legal knowledge he possessed, however, he still managed to draft a faulty trust to which he improperly transferred title of his house. This transfer later resulted in him losing the ownership of his home; he tried to refinance his home and discovered he no longer owned it because the faulty trust had ownership. In the end, it cost him thousands to fix the problem rather than simply doing it right the first time.

It is dangerously easy to lose control of your assets when you start dabbling on your own with quitclaim deeds, trusts, and other estate-planning documents. This con helps to emphasize the fact that the type of attorney you consult with really does matter.

No One Is Available to Counsel You on the Right Path for Your Situation

Everyone's situation is unique. There are many different documents that can help you plan for every situation that arises, but you have to know what those documents are, how to properly draft them, and how to use them. With the right attorney, you get sound advice and a sound plan. If you have questions, they get answered immediately. It is difficult to make a plan work if you don't fully understand how it operates, so ask away!

It Could Cost You More in the Long Run

If you draft a plan that ends up not working or leads to litigation, your family members could incur fees in the tens of thousands or hundreds of thousands of dollars. Contesting a will is *not* cheap. **It's safe to say that if your plan leads to litigation, the lawyers—rather than your children—will be getting your estate.**

If a mistake is realized before you pass away, the cost to fix a self-created problem is much higher than the cost to put a solid plan in place now with an experienced lawyer.

It All Depends on What You Want

If what you care about is the security of knowing that what you have will work when the time comes, then hiring a lawyer is the right move for you. If you want peace of mind knowing that everything has been taken care of and that someone will be around to make sure your plan goes smoothly, then hiring a lawyer is the right choice.

If all you really want is a list of property on a sheet of paper designating who gets what—and you don't care about the issues mentioned above—then a do-it-yourself plan may be perfect for you. If you simply do not have the cash to pay a lawyer, then a do-it-yourself plan may be necessary.

Cost can play a big factor in whether or not people get a plan drafted by a lawyer. At first glance, it does not seem "cheap" to hire a lawyer. When compared to the alternative costs of what could happen if things are done improperly, however, the initial fee to hire a lawyer is small, regardless of how large an estate you have.

At Least Do a Free Consultation

Most lawyers are available for a free consultation to discuss your options. **At the very least, please pursue this route.** A lawyer may be willing to guide you so you can get something in place. In the end, you care about your family and making sure your things end up in the right place. You are reading this book, so you clearly want to be informed and make sure things line up correctly. The best way to ensure that happens is to have a professional walk you through the process.

It would be great if everyone could just have a full understanding of the law without having attended law school and passing a multi-day bar exam. The bottom line is that you pay a professional to know what you don't know. Someone with proper knowledge who knows the pitfalls and missteps and how to avoid them. Someone who can give you peace of mind that your plan will work so you can stop worrying and rest easy. When you hire the right estate-planning lawyer, you not only get the documents you need, you get the peace of mind you deserve.

Appendix

The appendix to this guide is a one-stop shop for important review documents, as well as items that can get you started putting your important information into one place. While you prepare to have a complete estate plan, the documents in this appendix will help you stay organized. Should anything happen to you, these documents will help those you leave behind.

Please feel free to copy them and use them as you wish.

Included in this appendix:

- Larger Breakdown of Documents and Certain Topics Discussed
- Estate Planning FAQ
- Estate Planning Common Terms
- Important Contact Information Sheet
- Important-Papers Checklist

Larger Breakdown of Documents

Note: All numbers relate to Colorado laws as of 2018.

Will

1. Lets you say where you want your stuff to go when you die.
2. Lets you name a guardian for your children.
3. Allows you to name a personal representative to run the probate process.

Trust

1. Lets you say where you want your stuff to go when you die.
2. Protects your stuff and your family immediately—not later, like a will.
3. Allows you to avoid probate (unlike a will).

Guardianship

1. Allows you to name an individual or set of people to care for your children if you can't anymore.
2. Is the best way to prevent your children from going to foster care should something happen to you.

Financial Power of Attorney

1. Designates an individual to manage your money and assets if you can't anymore.

2. Prevents the court from appointing a professional, called a conservator, to manage your assets.

Medical Power of Attorney

1. Designates an individual to talk to doctors and make medical decisions for you if you can't anymore.
2. Prevents the court from appointing a professional, called a guardian, to manage your health-care decisions.

Living Will

1. Allows you to choose how many days you would like to be on life support in an end-of-life situation.
2. Takes that extremely stressful, difficult decision out of your family's hands.

Probate

1. Is the process individuals go through after passing away in order to transfer title of their assets to their heirs.
2. Is not necessary if you have less than $66,000 in your name alone (this number changes each year) and do not own any real estate. It is also not necessary if you have a properly funded trust.

Health Insurance Portability and Accountability Act (HIPAA) Release

1. Allows you to name those whom you want to have access to your medical records.

2. Allows the named individuals to be in the room with your doctor and medical power of attorney when they are speaking about your health.

Personal Property Memorandum (PPM)

1. Lets you itemize any personal property, like family heirlooms, that you want to leave to specific people.

2. Prevents you from having a new will signing every time you change your mind about your personal property and whom you want to receive it.

Declaration of Final Remains Document

1. Allows you to state how you want to be treated regarding being buried or cremated.

2. Allows you to state if you would prefer to have a funeral or memorial service.

Irrevocable Trust

1. Has the same benefits as a trust but, in complex family situations, it is mainly used to avoid estate-tax issues or to guarantee that specific individuals will inherit after you are gone.

2. Cannot be revoked.

Delegation of Parental Rights

1. Allows you to assign an individual your rights as a parent in case you are not able to be present for a certain

period of time. (This is different than a guardianship for your minor children because you are still alive with this tool in effect.)

Estate Planning FAQ

What is estate planning?

Estate planning involves creating a plan for loved ones on how to distribute property when you pass away. It is also used to create guardianships for children, assign powers of attorney over your finances/health care should you become incapacitated, and obtain tax advantages by avoiding gift and estate tax.

What happens if I do not have a will or estate plan?

If you do not have an estate plan, your property will pass according to your state's intestacy laws. These laws can apply even if you had verbal agreements with individuals regarding the distribution of your property.

Doesn't my spouse take over my things without an estate plan?

Not necessarily. Certain things will transfer to your spouse automatically, such as jointly owned property, but there may be financial and health-care decisions that your spouse will not be able to make without a proper power of attorney.

How long is the process?

Every estate plan is different, so determining the length of time is unique for each client. For a basic estate plan, the process can take less than one month to complete. For more complicated plans, the process can be much longer.

How often do I need to update my plan?

It is always a good idea to review your plan when any red-flag events happen, like marriages, divorces, new additions to the family, or deaths in the family. This way, you and your attorney can accommodate for any changes and plan accordingly. A good rule of thumb is to look over your plan at least every five years, if not more often.

What is probate and why is avoiding probate beneficial for me?

Probate is the court process of transferring title of assets to the correct beneficiaries after death. This process is public and can be costly and time-consuming if no plan is in place. Avoiding probate can allow your heirs to avoid court costs and attorney fees if done right. It also allows them to receive assets sooner and keep the process private. There are pros and cons to avoiding probate, and each person's situation is unique.

Estate Planning Common Terms

Will

A will is the most basic estate-planning tool available. It is a document that allows you to decide who will receive your property and how your final affairs should be handled. It also allows you to name guardians for your minor children and appoint a personal representative (formerly called an executor) to run the probate process after you pass. If you don't have this document, the state will create a plan for you and you won't get to decide who gets your things.

Trust

A trust is a document created by an individual (called the trustor or settlor) that gives property to a trustee to hold and manage for the benefit of others (beneficiaries). This is similar to a will in that it can allow an individual to provide for others after they pass. The difference is that a trust can take effect immediately and allows the trustor/settlor to avoid probate.

Guardianship

A guardian is a person put in place to care for another (a ward). He or she owes special duties to the ward as well as the court. Guardians make educational and medical decisions for the ward, as well as decide where the ward will live. A guardian may also be given the power to manage the ward's assets.

Power of Attorney

This document allows you to assign individuals to handle your affairs should you become incapacitated. A medical power of attorney makes medical decisions on your behalf, while a financial power of attorney makes decisions regarding your assets and money. If you don't have a power of attorney and are in an accident, your family may have to enter an expensive guardianship and conservatorship hearing with the court to name this person for you.

Living Will

Also known as an "advance health-care directive," this document allows you to designate how long you wish to remain on life support in an end-of-life situation.

Pet Trust

This is a type of honorary trust that allows you to leave money behind to a caregiver who can only use that money to provide for a comfortable life for your pet.

Charitable Trust

This type of trust allows you to fund your favorite charities while also helping to obtain tax advantages and support your family.

Probate

Probate is a court process that individuals must go through to distribute any property that is titled solely in the name of the deceased and pay off any creditors of the deceased's estate. Many individuals create estate plans to avoid probate and the costs associated with it.

Contact Sheet
Important Contact Information

I recommend prioritizing these contacts so your children or agent will know whom to contact first in case of an emergency.

Local Relatives

Name: _____

Phone: _____

Email: _____

Local Relatives

Name: _____

Phone: _____

Email: _____

Local Relatives

Name: _____

Phone: _____

Email: _____

Minister/Priest/Rabbi

Name: _____

Phone: _____

Email: _____

Physician

Name: _____

Phone: _____

Email: _____

Attorney

Name: _____

Phone: _____

Email: _____

Accountant

Name: _____

Phone: _____

Email: _____

Financial Planner

Name: _____

Phone: _____

Email: _____

Life Insurance Representative

Name: _____

Phone: _____

Email: _____

Stock Broker

Name: _____

Phone: _____

Email: _____

Other Key Contacts

Name: _____

Phone: _____

Email: _____

Relationship: _____

Other Key Contacts

Name: _____

Phone: _____

Email: _____

Relationship: _____

Other Key Contacts

Name: _____

Phone: _____

Email: _____

Relationship: _____

Important-Papers Checklist

I strongly recommend that this document be password protected if kept in digital format. If it is printed, I strongly encourage you to keep it in a locked, fireproof safe. If this information gets into the wrong hands, it could cause serious financial and emotional damage to everyone involved. By filling out this document, you agree to hold Althaus Law LLC and Jeff Althaus harmless for any and all damages incurred, if any should arise.

Estate-Planning Documents	Location/Info
Will	_____
Trust	_____
Financial Power of Attorney	_____
Medical Power of Attorney	_____
HIPAA Release	_____
Living Will	_____
Final-Arrangements Document	_____
Insurance Policies	
Health	_____
Life	_____
Long-Term Care	_____

Accident   _____

Homeowners   _____

Auto   _____

Business   _____

Other   _____

Personal Papers

Birth Certificate   _____

Children's Birth Certificates   _____

Social Security Cards   _____

Citizenship Papers   _____

Adoption Papers   _____

Divorce Records   _____

Military Documents   _____

Safe-Deposit Box & Key   _____

Safe Combination   _____

Other   _____

Bank and Tax Information

Income Tax Returns   _____

Bank Statements   _____

Checkbook _____

Other _____

Business Documents

Incorporation Papers _____

Partnership Agreements _____

Other _____

Assets/Investments

Stocks _____

Mutual Funds _____

Bonds _____

Keogh Plans and IRAs _____

Annuity Contracts _____

Retirement Plans _____

Profit-Sharing Plans _____

Stock Options _____

Other Investments _____

Notes/Loans _____

Rental Properties _____

Other _____

Deeds and Titles

Real Estate   _____

Motor Vehicles   _____

Other Personal Property   _____

Burial Documents

Instructions   _____

Cemetery Plot Deed   _____

Burial Insurance   _____

Others

_____   _____

_____   _____

_____   _____

_____   _____

_____   _____

_____   _____

_____   _____

_____   _____

Resources

1) Lumpkins Walls, Barbranda. "Survey: 60% of Americans Lack Will or Estate Planning." AARP. Accessed September 3, 2018. https://www.aarp.org/money/investing/info-2017/half-of-adults-do-not-have-wills.html.

2) Kennedy, A.L.. "Statistics on Last Wills & Testaments." LegalZoom. Accessed September 3, 2018.https://info.legalzoom.com/statistics-last-wills-testaments-3947.html.

3) Lumpkins Walls, Barbranda. "Haven't Done a Will Yet?." AARP. Accessed September 3, 2018. https://www.aarp.org/money/investing/info-2017/half-of-adults-do-not-have-wills.html.

4) Volkov, Sasha. "Rocket Lawyer Survey Reveals a Majority of Americans Do Not Have a Will." Accessed September 3, 2018. http://www.marketwired.com/press-release/rocket-lawyer-survey-reveals-a-majority-of-americans-do-not-have-a-will-1420402.html.

5) Greenhough, Jenny. "Will Power! New Infographic." Accessed September 3, 2018. https://www.rocketlawyer.com/blog/got-will-power-new-infographic-95252.

6) Baldyga, Mike. "Nearly Two-Thirds of Americans Don't Have Living Wills -- Do You?." Accessed September 3, 2018. http://newsroom.acep.org/2016-03-21-Nearly-Two-Thirds-of-Americans-Dont-Have-Living-Wills-Do-You.